VIKING  R

MW00563196

THE BRITISH MUSEUM
VIKING POETRY
OF LOVE AND WAR

Judith Jesch

For Tom

© 2013 The Trustees of
the British Museum

Judith Jesch has asserted the right to
be identified as the author of this work

First published in 2013 by
The British Museum Press
A division of
The British Museum Company Ltd
38 Russell Square, London WC1B 3QQ
britishmuseum.org/publishing

ISBN 978 0 7141 2830 6

Designed by James Alexander,
JADE Design
Printed in China by Toppan Leefung
Printed Limited

The papers used by the British
Museum Press are recyclable products
and the manufacturing processes
are expected to conform to the
environmental regulations of the
country of origin.

The majority of artworks illustrated
in this book are from the collection
of the British Museum and are © The
Trustees of the British Museum. The
registration numbers for these objects
are provided in the corresponding
captions. To find out more about
these and objects in all areas of the
British Museum's collection, visit:
britishmuseum.org/research/search_
the_collection_database.aspx

Frontispiece William Walker (1729–
93), King Athelstan saving the life of
his father, Edward the Elder, at the
Battle of Sherwood, by taking Leofrid
the Dane prisoner. Etching and
engraving (print on paper), London,
1786. 24.8 x 16.3 cm. British Museum
1872,1109.79.

Contents

7   Introduction

18   **Scenes of battle**

36   **In praise of warriors**

52   **A life under sail**

62   **Love and lust**

76   **Goddesses and valkyries**

90   **Love and hate**

104   Biographical notes
106   Mythological names
108   Geographical names
109   Further reading
111   Picture credits

Introduction

The Vikings are more renowned for war than for poetry, let alone love, yet they had a keen and overlapping interest in all three. Although not often thought of as poets, they came from a culture that valued poetry highly and rewarded poets handsomely. For them the main function of poetry was to record and to celebrate. In an oral culture, the fixed structures of their poetry enabled the remembering and transmission of information about the glorious deeds of sailors and warriors, and were a useful form of propaganda for chieftains and kings, both alive and dead. Poetry also served as a repository of stories about gods and heroes, expressed the ups and downs of daily life, including relations between the sexes, and mediated between the human and the divine worlds. As keen warriors whose code centred on the mythological female figure of the valkyrie (see p. 107), the Vikings were quick to see both the similarities and the differences between love and war, and the two are sometimes hard to separate in their poetry.

The themes of this poetry are mythological, military and memorial; there is also a small set of distinctive love poems which encompasses both native traditions and literary influences from further south. The tone of the poetry ranges from the highly formal to the scurrilous, and it is often light-hearted, even in the face of death and tragedy.

It is possible to document a continuous, thousand-year long, poetical tradition in northern Europe, and especially Scandinavia, from the fifth century AD to around 1500, spanning the whole of the Viking Age (c.800–1100) as well

Vikings cross the English Channel and prepare to attack Angers, France. The attack took place in the 9th century, although the Viking warriors are here depicted in armour of a later time, c.1100, when the manuscript was made. Illustration from the manuscript *La Vie de Saint Aubin d'Angers*. Vellum, c.1080–1100, Anjou, France. 29.5 x 20.4 cm. Bibliothèque Nationale, Paris, Ms. Nouv. acq. Lat. 1390, fol. 7.

as several centuries either side. This continuity is matched by a linguistic continuity, at least from the Viking Age to the end of the Middle Ages (*c.*1500), which enables us to speak of the language as 'Old Norse' throughout. This long-term poetical tradition is based on the alliterative long line, a fundamental structure in all Germanic poetry, which was then developed in the Old Norse tradition in various ways during the Viking Age and after.

Some early runic inscriptions reveal the same poetical forms as are found in later medieval manuscripts, but in the Viking Age poetry was primarily an oral form, and has to be reconstructed from those later manuscripts. From the twelfth century onwards, Iceland – a Norse colony established in the Viking Age – became the guardian and repository of the traditional poetry of the Scandinavian peoples. At this time, poetry made the significant transition from orality to literacy, with the Icelandic antiquarians consciously recording their inherited traditions, ensuring their survival to the present day. Important texts from the thirteenth century onwards are the *Poetic Edda*, the *Prose Edda* of the Icelandic historian, poet and politician Snorri Sturluson (1179–1241), and many sagas (long historical narratives –some of them also by Snorri), and it is from these that most of the poems in this book are taken.

Old Norse poetry from around 800 onwards can conveniently be divided into two main genres: 'Eddic' and 'skaldic'. Eddic poetry takes its name from the anthology known as the *Poetic Edda*, found primarily in one late

William Gershom Collingwood (1854–1932), *The Parliament of Ancient Iceland.* Watercolour painting, British, *c.*1897. 90 x 69.5 cm. British Museum OA.10759.

thirteenth-century manuscript known as the *Codex Regius* (King's Book) because it was presented to the king of Denmark by an Icelandic bishop in the seventeenth century. This manuscript contains poems of mythological and legendary character, composed at various times and in various places. The prehistory of the manuscript can be traced back to about 1200, so the poems are certainly at least that old, but how much older than that is difficult to tell. It is clear that much of the material in the *Poetic Edda* – the stories of the pagan gods and legendary heroes, the conceptual vocabulary, the ideologies and beliefs – is of great antiquity, since many of the stories told there have archaeological and art-historical parallels from much earlier periods (pp. 92–95). However, the poems themselves may well be reworkings of older versions, as their structures are quite loose and it is hard to imagine them remaining unchanged in the oral tradition for many centuries.

Skaldic poetry, by contrast, is designed to be remembered accurately in an oral culture, and has much tighter metrical and linguistic structures to enable this. While all Germanic poetry (including Eddic poetry) makes use of alliteration as a main structuring principle, skaldic poetry adds to this a stanzaic format, strict syllable counting, internal rhyme and a complex diction based on kennings (explained on pp. 14–16) to produce a tightly-woven poetry that once learned could not be forgotten. The heyday of this poetry was in the tenth and eleventh centuries, towards the end of the Viking Age, and it is richly represented in this collection. A feature almost universally absent from this type of poetry is end-rhyme. The one exception is Egil Skallagrimsson's poem in praise of Eirik 'Bloodaxe' (p. 39), composed and performed in York.

When the medieval authors of Iceland began writing the long historical narratives known as sagas, many of which were set in the Viking Age, they naturally turned to this form of poetry as both source and inspiration. For these Icelandic authors, the skaldic stanzas sprinkled throughout their texts provided authentication and authenticity, as well as enabling an exciting new style of writing, the *prosimetrum*, in which fairly straightforward narrative prose was interspersed with the elaborate intricacies of skaldic verse. In these contexts the poems functioned either as footnotes, citing the author's sources, or as direct quotations – utterances spoken by characters in the story as part of the action.

Unlike Eddic poetry, skaldic poetry is normally located in a specific historical context. While Eddic poetry is anonymous, most skaldic poetry is preserved with a poet's name attached; indeed the word 'skaldic' comes from Old Norse *skald*, meaning 'poet'. The poet is the guarantor of the authenticity of the information in the poem, but also the creative figure who requires payment for his propagandistic services from the object of his praise, who is then the poet's 'generous friend' (p. 56). The poet is also often a figure in his own poetry, not quite the lyric self of the Romantics, but certainly desiring to express his own feelings and experiences to the world. Eddic poetry, on the other hand, is based on stories that were common currency, myths and legends of gods and heroes that were familiar to all. We may detect the individual poetic voices behind some Eddic poems, but we have no idea who these people were. Some of these anonymous poets could well have been women, and several Eddic poems reflect a clearly female perspective (p. 96). Even skaldic poetry is occasionally attributed to a female speaker (p. 62). However, the poetry of record, by official court poets, and celebrating the deeds of kings and chieftains, was largely a masculine, and elite, genre. Kings and earls could be poets, too, though their productions are generally more casual and occasional (pp. 28, 32, 35, 64, 67, 80, 88).

The language of Viking poetry is colourful, intricate and steeped in mythological knowledge. A particular feature is the *kenning*, a complex form of metaphorical diction that introduces new and often bizarrely incongruous imagery. In the early thirteenth century, the great Icelander Snorri Sturluson (1179–1241) recognized that this type of poetry was going out of fashion and becoming more difficult for his younger contemporaries to understand. He therefore composed his *Edda*, also known as the *Prose Edda*, to explain the forms and structures of skaldic poetry. (The name *Edda* in fact properly belongs to Snorri's work, but it was extended to the *Poetic Edda* in the seventeenth century in recognition of the overlaps between the two.) As well as explaining skaldic poetry, Snorri at the same time invaluably cited many examples of it which had not made their way into the sagas. He also provided a handy summary of Old Norse mythology – knowledge of which was essential to understanding the diction of skaldic poetry – again citing many stanzas of poems known from the *Poetic Edda*, but also some not found there, such as the dialogue between Njord and Skadi (p. 91).

Even before the Icelanders decided to fix their poetical traditions in writing, the runic alphabet was used elsewhere in the Viking world for the same purpose. Thus there are short poems in both Eddic and skaldic style to be found inscribed in runes on stone, bone and wood from both the Viking Age and after, and a few of these texts have been included in this book. These inscriptions, particularly the earliest ones, are important contemporary evidence for the poetry of the Viking Age, and help to sustain the argument that the poetry recorded in later Icelandic manuscripts also had its roots in that period. The runic verse ranges from the monumental commemoration of the dead, just as in skaldic verse, to the throwaway lines carved on sticks of wood in the taverns of medieval Bergen in Norway.

The translation of Old Norse poetry is not for the faint-hearted. Skaldic poetry is often intentionally, Eddic poetry probably unintentionally, obscure. There are many unfamiliar names to puzzle the uninformed reader (these are listed and explained on pp. 104–108). The greatest difficulty for the reader is in understanding the kennings, simple versions of which are found in Eddic poetry, but which are abundant and most obvious in skaldic poetry. A kenning is basically a figure of speech, often though not necessarily metaphorical, which denotes some person or thing in terms of something else with which it is not usually associated. The classic example is when a camel is called 'ship of the desert'. A camel is not a ship, and the desert is not the sea, far from it. However the camel is the mode of transport appropriate to the desert, just as the ship is the mode of transport appropriate to the sea. The image works particularly well because the rolling dunes of the desert are not unlike the waves of the sea and the rocking ride on a camel like the rocking motion of a boat. The Vikings were not familiar with camels, but had exactly the same idea in reverse when they called a ship a 'sea's steed' (p. 56) or a 'bay-horse' (p. 60), which is nothing to do with its colour but everything to do with the fact that it helps you across the bay.

These roundabout figures of speech were sometimes taken further and often involved mythological knowledge. So both men and women were conceptualized as trees (making use of the fact that different tree-names could be grammatically either masculine or feminine), and these trees were identified as people by the association with weapons (for men) and jewellery (for women). Similarly, the names of gods and goddesses could be used as the base-words in kennings for men and women, in both cases

Silver from the Viking hoard buried around 905–10 and found at Cuerdale, Lancashire, in 1840. Weight 1.65 g. British Museum 1838,0710.1203. Donated by Queen Victoria.

linked back to the human world by the objects with which they were associated (e.g. 'sword-Odin', p. 43, and 'Gunn of fine linen', p. 59). Such woman-kennings provide the names of a lot of otherwise completely obscure goddesses – to avoid overloading the translations with strange names, I have sometimes simply translated as 'goddess'.

The standard kenning-types such as these quickly become familiar, but then there are some really obscure ones, such as when Egil denotes summer by the kenning 'valley-fish relief' (p. 19), the 'valley-fish' being a snake, and its 'relief' the warmth of summertime. Translating every kenning literally would not only have made the translator's task nearly impossible, but also disadvantaged the reader who does not have the full background knowledge required to decode these riddles. But kennings are such an important part of the poetry, especially skaldic poetry, that I have translated as many as possible, providing brief explanations below each text.

Another difficulty for the translator is that of metre and structure. Both Eddic and skaldic verse can use a range of different metres, and the reader who is interested in the detail of this can find information in the books listed in Further reading (pp. 109–110). I have tried to echo these metres in my translations, without striving for a full fidelity which would be impossible, especially in the strictly syllable-counting skaldic metres. My translations also make use of alliteration and internal rhyme where possible, though it has not been possible to implement this according to the rules of the Old Norse poetry.

Another striking aspect of skaldic poetry in particular is the unnatural word-order. This is an unavoidable result of the structures of this poetry, in which various forms of rhyme and alliteration have to be accommodated in strictly-defined places within the 48-syllable stanza. Such jumbled word order would not be possible in modern English, where meaning in a sentence is largely determined by word order. But Old Norse is an inflected language in which it is possible to reconstruct the correct structure of the sentence from the endings of the words – another factor which contributes to the riddle-like quality of skaldic verse. The translator cannot replicate all of these peculiarities of Old Norse poetry exactly, but I have endeavoured to give a flavour of all of them in my versions.

Egil Skallagrimsson (10th century)
The poet encourages his fellows to attack the town of Lund

Reddener of the wolf's tooth,
let's hold gleaming swords high,
we've got deeds to perform
in valley-fish relief.
Every man up to Lund,
as quickly as he can!
Let's chant the song of spears
before the sun goes down.

reddener of the wolf's tooth = warrior; *valley-fish* = snake, its *relief* = summertime; *song of spears* = battle

'Hogsback' monument (detail) showing two bands of warriors approaching each other. Red sandstone, England, first half of 10th century. 167.6 x 28.6 x 66 cm (maximum dimensions). St Mary's Church, Gosforth, Cumbria.

Egil Skallagrimsson
(10th century)
The poet remembers
battles in Sweden

I went with bloody sword
(wound-grouse following me)
and a resounding spear
to a hard viking attack.
We had a raging fight,
fire raced over houses;
I made bloody bodies
fall within city walls.

wound-grouse = raven

Viking sword. Silver, iron and copper,
England, 10th century. Length 88.5 cm.
British Museum 1887,0209.1. Bequeathed by
Henry Dunbar Baines.

*Egil Skallagrimsson
(10th century)*

The poet tells of fighting for
King Athelstan in England

I piled the field with corpses
round banners in the west,
in fearsome fight I attacked
Earl Adils with steel-blue Snake.
Young King Olaf had three steel-
clashes with the English;
Earl Hring held a weapon-moot,
the ravens did not starve.

Snake = the name of Egil's sword;
steel-clashes = battle; *weapon-moot* = battle

Silver penny issued by Olaf
Guthfrithsson, Hiberno-Norse
king of York. The coin depicts a
raven on the obverse and a cross
on the reverse. Minted in York,
England, 939–41. Diameter 20 mm.
British Museum 1915,0507.768.

Anonymous (11th century)

A Viking tells a woman of the capture of London

Every day Hogni's door
became quite bloody, goddess,
when we fought in the fray,
early, with our leader.
Since hard-fought fight is now
finished, we can sit in
fair London, o land
of the sun of the sea.

Hogni's door = shield; *sun of the sea* = gold,
its *land* = woman

John Wykeham Archer (1808–64), drawing of
a runic monument found on the south side of
St Paul's Cathedral, London. Watercolour on
graphite, Britain, 1852. 24.7 x 34.6 cm. British
Museum 1874,0314.318.

Arnor Thordarson
(11th century)
Thorfinn Sigurdarson,
Earl of Orkney, makes a foray into England

The earl bore his banner
on to ancient English ground,
his troop reddened eagle's tongue
as he made flags advance.
Flames shot up; halls collapsed;
his men made refugees;
the foe of boughs spewed smoke
and threw light towards the sky.

redden eagle's tongue = provide the eagle with
carrion in the form of corpses; *foe of boughs* = fire

Sébastien Leclerc (1637–1714), Norse attacking
a convent in England, with monks running
away. Book illustration (print on paper),
French, *c.*1705. 8 x 14 cm. British Museum
1917,1208.71.199. Donated by Nan Ino Cooper,
Baroness Lucas of Crudwell and Lady Dingwall,
in Memory of Auberon Thomas Herbert, 9th
Baron Lucas of Crudwell and 5th Lord Dingwall.

Harald Sigurdarson,
king of Norway (11th century)
The young Harald escapes from the
battle of Stiklestad (1030), in which
the farmers of Norway killed his
half-brother King Olaf Haraldsson

I remained upright
in battle while wounds bled;
the farmers' troop grew fuller,
destroyer of shields dealt death.
Now, with little glory
I slink through the forests;
who knows, whether I'll become
widely famous later?

destroyer of shields = sword

The Death of King Warwolf, after Frederick Sandys
(1829–1904). Woodblock print on paper, British,
1862. 14.1 x 11.5 cm. British Museum 1927,0419.6.

Grani (11th century)
King Harald feeds the beasts of battle

The prince made the eaglets
a drink of Danish blood;
he made a Christmas meal
for Gudenå's ravens;
the eagle's children trampled
all over the corpses;
the wolf ate Jutish meat,
well may it smack its lips!

Silver disc brooch. Sutton, Cambridgeshire,
England, early 11th century. Diameter 14.9 cm.
British Museum 1951,1011.1.

Harald Sigurdarson, king of Norway
(11th century)
Harald is caught unawares at the battle
of Stamford Bridge (1066) and has to fight
without armour

We're advancing, in serried ranks,
mail-coatless, under steel-blue blades.
Helmets are shining, but I haven't got mine,
our armour is down with the ships.

Picture stone with runic inscription, depicting
a warrior on Odin's eight-legged horse being
received into Valhalla, and a ship full of armed
warriors. Limestone (red paint modern). Gotland,
Sweden, 9th/10th century. Height 175 cm.
National Historical Museum, Stockholm.

Harald Sigurdarson, king of Norway (11th century)
Shortly before his death at Stamford Bridge, Harald remembers his mother's advice

Faithful falcon-field goddess
commanded this of me:
not to creep behind the shield
in the noise of weapons.
The necklace-support told me
to hold my helmet-base high
where valkyrie-ice and skulls
meet in the clash of metal.

falcon-field = arm, its *goddess* = woman; *noise of weapons* = battle; *necklace-support* = woman; *helmet-base* = head; *valkyrie-ice* = sword; *clash of metal* = battle

Beserkers (Norse warriors) from the Lewis Chessmen. Walrus ivory chess pieces, probably made in Norway, *c.*1150–1175; found on the Isle of Lewis, Scotland. Heights (from left) 8.5 cm, 9.2 cm and 8.2 cm. British Museum 1831,1101.123.

Anonymous (11th century),
Gripsholm rune stone
Ingvar and his men die far away
from Sweden

They journeyed boldly,
went far for gold,
fed the eagle
out in the east,
and died in the south
in Saracenland.

Rune stone from the grounds of Gripsholm
Castle, Södermanland, Sweden, 11th century.
Granite. Height 200 cm.

Egil Skallagrimsson (10th century)
The poet praises King Eirik 'Bloodaxe'
Haraldsson for his warlike deeds

Sword-edges clashed
and arrowheads bashed,
from all that came
King Eirik's fame.

Reddened sword he drew,
ravens got to chew,
arrows hit a few,
bloody spears flew.
He made Scots bleed
witches' mounts to feed.
Nari's sister stood
on the eagle's food.

witches' mounts = wolves; *Nari's sister* = Hel, goddess of
the dead; *eagle's food* = carrion, corpses

Obverse of silver penny issued by King Eric.
Minted in York, England, 947–54. Diameter
2.1 cm. British Museum E.5081.

Anonymous (10th century)
King Eirik 'Bloodaxe' is expected in Valhalla

Odin:
What a dream! I dreamt I woke at dawn
to tidy Valhalla for the fallen ones;
I woke the Einherjar, made them get up
to cover the benches and wash the cups,
made the Valkyries bring wine, as a prince was coming.
I'm expecting some renowned heroes
from the human world; my heart is glad!
What's that rumble, Bragi, like thousands marching,
or a massive movement?

Bragi:
The creaking of the benches sounds like Baldr
is coming home to Odin's hall.

Odin:
Bragi, you're way too wise to talk such rubbish,
and you know very well,
it's all booming for Eirik, the prince is coming
to Odin's hall.

Hack-silver, coins and ingots from the Viking hoard
known as the Vale of York Hoard, which was buried in
the 920s and found in North Yorkshire, England in 2007.
British Museum 2009,8023.1–76 and 2009,4133.77–693.
Jointly acquired with the York Museums Trust.

Kveld-Ulf Bjalfason (10th century)
The poet laments the loss of his son Thorolf

Now I've heard that Thorolf
met his end in the north,
the Norn is fierce to me,
the sword-Odin fell too soon.
Heaviness of age keeps me
from the moot of metal's
goddess; revenge will be slow,
though my mind is eager.

sword-Odin = warrior; *metal's goddess* = valkyrie,
her *moot* = battle

Bone plaque or button, with a design of a man
(head missing) with legs turned up and joined
to body by two interlaced animals. Anglo-
Scandinavian, late 10th century, found in London.
Diameter 6 cm. British Museum 1866,0224.1.
Donated by Sir Augustus Wollaston Franks.

Glass drinking horn. Germany, 5th century.
Length 34.1 cm. British Museum 1873,0502.212.
Bequeathed by Felix Slade.

Arnor Thordarson (11th century)
The heroic deeds of King Magnus 'the Good'
Olafsson provide the poet with material

Olaf's avenger, you got me
my material – I made it speak.
You let Hlokk's hawks drink corpse-liquid,
so my eulogy can grow.

Olaf (Haraldsson)'s avenger = Magnus; *Hlokk* = a valkyrie,
her *hawks* = carrion birds; *corpse-liquid* = blood

Arnor Thordarson (11th century)
King Magnus kills many on a military
expedition to the Baltic

The brisk prince piled barley
of wolves in a heap so high
(I praise the captain of men,
his conscientious life)
that the river-bone god's
wife's steed couldn't climb it
when roaming round at night;
corpses lay far and wide.

barley of wolves = food for wolves, carrion; *river-bone* =
stone, its *god* = giant, his *wife* = giantess, her *steed* = wolf

Gravestone, tapered and carved on one side,
with two moustached human masks at ends of
foliate interlace, and two animal heads at the
other end. Bibury, Gloucestershire, England,
Anglo-Scandinavian, 11th century.
Height 63.5 cm. British Museum 1913,0203.1.
Donated by Rev. F. G. Dutton.

Arnor Thordarson (11th century)
The youthful career of Thorfinn
Sigurdarson, Earl of Orkney

The ruler reddened sword-blades
in the storm of helmets;
he bloodied Hugin's feet
before he was fifteen.
There was none younger under
cloud-hall than Einar's brother
ready to defend his land
and boldly to attack.

storm of helmets = battle; *cloud-hall* = the sky,
under it = on earth

Harald I Finehair (*c.*890–*c.*946) receiving the
kingdom of Norway from his father Halfdan the
Black. Illustration (detail) from the manuscript
Flateyjarbók. Icelandic, *c.*1390. Árni Magnússon
Institute, Reykjavík, GKS 1005 fol.

Arnor Thordarson (11th century)
The final verdict on Thorfinn,
Earl of Orkney

Bright sun will become black,
earth will sink into dark sea,
Austri's burden will break,
waves will cover mountains,
before a better chieftain
than Thorfinn will be raised
in these isles; may God help
that liege of his hall-troop.

Austri's burden = the sky; *these isles* = Orkney and Shetland

Cast silver disc brooch, covered in interlace
and with three-dimensional animal and human
figures. Gotland, Sweden (?), 10th century.
Diameter 7.8 cm. British Museum 1901,0718.1.
Donated by Friends of the British Museum.

Reverse of a ten-shilling banknote depicting a
Viking ship. Isle of Man, Great Britain. 13.8 x
6.5 cm. British Museum 1985,0735.149.

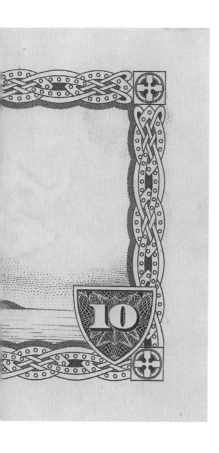

Egil Skallagrimsson (10th century)
The six-year-old poet looks forward
to a life as a Viking

My mother said to me
that they would buy for me
a ship and lovely oars
to go away with vikings,
standing in the stern,
steering the glorious ship,
then putting into ports,
killing a man or two.

Thjodolf Arnorsson (11th century)
King Harald's war-fleet is launched
from the River Nid in Trondheim

Fair lady, I saw the ship launched
from the river into the sea.
See where the long-sided warship
lies, splendid, off the shore.
The bright dragon's mane above
the cargo shines, since he was launched
from rollers, his decorated
neck is burnished with gold.

The troop-lord casts off the long
cover on Saturday,
where splendid widows from the
city see the dragon's side.
The young king steers the new ship
westwards out of the Nid
while the oars of the sailors
splash into the sea.

The prince's band can pull
their oars straight out of the sea.
The widow looks and admires
the wondrous flight of the oars.
Lady, there'll be much rowing
till the tarred sea-tools fall apart.
The four-edged pine allows that
while there is still full peace.

sea-tools = oars; *four-edged pine* = oar

Illustration (detail) of the constellation Argo,
taken from *Cicero's Aratus*. Vellum, originally
produced in Winchester, England, second
quarter of 11th century. British Library, London,
Cotton Tiberius B. V. Part 1, f.40v.

Post canis igitur magni cauda scd
constituta é quâ fabule poetarû ĩ a stra
mi   nerua que primú ea excogitasse
             muitum fuerat hominibꝫ: prîu
             habet autem stellas   ĩ pupe
             mo mali. ĩ subcarī   na

stellaru ordin
collocata du
dicit. et ĩ nare
nduali ĩgen
iiii. ĩ latere:
v. sunt. xvii.

A   udá serpens plabitur argo.
Conuerans pse portans cumlumine puppim.

Arnor Thordarson (11th century)
King Magnus 'the Good' Olafsson
and his ship 'Bison'

Giver of captured gold, you risked
your gazelles of the raging storm
on the churning sea, and you spent
your life mostly under soaked sails.
The 'Bison' quickly carried you,
a keen hawk, in its stern-quarters.
More splendid king will never steer
a supple ship, my generous friend.

When the ruler races his sea-skis
on the rolling slopes of Meiti,
it seems like an angel company
cruising for the Lord of Heaven.
The spoiler of the rough sea's steeds
is loved second only to God
by the people of this nation.
Your royalty remains forever.

gazelles of the storm = ships; *sea-skis* = ships; *slopes of Meiti*
(a sea-king) = sea; *sea's steeds* = ships

Sculpture, carved in relief with a depiction of the
Baptism of Christ. Walrus ivory, England, 10th–
11th century. Height 9.3 cm. British Museum
1974,1002.1. Purchased with contributions from
The Art Fund and Pilgrim Trust.

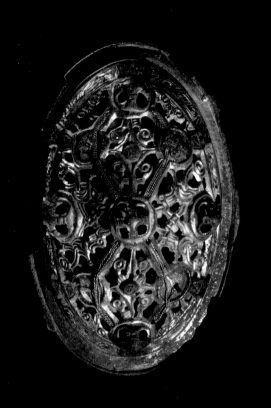
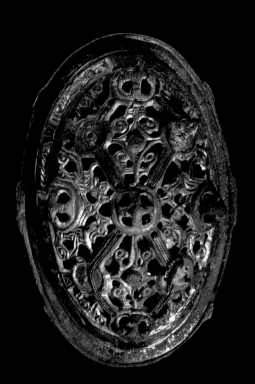

Hallfred Ottarsson (10th century)
The poet catches sight of his beloved,
Kolfinna

I thought, when I caught sight
of the Gunn of fine linen,
that a boat was floating
on the sea between two isles;
and the seam-Saga gleamed
amidst the stream of women,
like a well-equipped warship
with sail and golden tackle.

Gunn = a valkyrie; *fine linen* = headdress; *valkyrie of the
headdress* = (married) woman; *Saga* = a goddess; *goddess
of the seam* = woman

Pair of gilt bronze oval brooches, with silver
fittings and inlaid with silver wire. Downham,
Norfolk, England, late 9th to early 10th century.
Length 11.6 cm; width 7.9 cm. British Museum
1888,0103.1. Donated by Mrs W. Weller Poley.

Einar Skulason (12th century)
The poet admires the lady Ragnhildr
sailing out from Bergen

A valorous woman carves
the hollow wave with her prow
out to Utstein; the storm-driver
swells the sail above the yard.
No bay-horse on earth has
finer cargo on board;
planks of the broad-beamed ship
conquer the surging surf.

storm-driver = wind; *bay-horse* = ship

The Sea Stallion from Glendalough (a replica
of Skuldelev 2, an 11th-century warship built
in Dublin, Ireland but found near Roskilde,
Denmark) sailing near the west coast of
Scotland, July 2007.

Kormak Ogmundarson (10th century)
The poet and his beloved Steingerd reach
an understanding

Kormak:
Men ambush me to stop
me looking at your face,
but they'll have to take on
my weapon-island's snake,
for all big rivers will run
uphill, you shining bearer
of gleaming ale-vessels,
before I forsake you.

Who would you choose, linen-Hlin,
among the promoters
of the valkyrie's cause,
for your man? Your face shows it's me.

Steingerd:
Ring-giver, I'd betrothe myself
to Frodi's brother, were he blind,
gods and fate would be good to me,
in that case, whatever came.

weapon-island = shield; its *snake* = sword; *bearer of*
ale-vessels = woman; *linen-Hlin* (a goddess) = woman;
valkyrie's cause = battle; it's *promoter* = warrior;
ring-giver = (generous) man; *Frodi's brother* = Kormak

William Gershom Collingwood (1854–1932),
Steingerd glimpses Kormak. Detail from the
frontispiece (print on paper) of W. G. Collingwood
and Jon Stefansson, *The Life and Death of Cormac*
the Skald, Ulverston, England, 1902.

Olaf Haraldsson, king of Norway
(11th century)
Olaf laments the departure of the
Swedish princess Ingigerd Olafsdottir
to marry another

I stood on a mound, watching
a fair mount bear the woman,
the beautiful-eyed wife
caused me to lose pleasure.
Friendly woman, goddess of the
hawk's ground, quickly drove the horse
out of the yard; each man is
haunted by one mistake.

hawk's ground = arm, resting-place of the hawk,
its *goddess* = woman

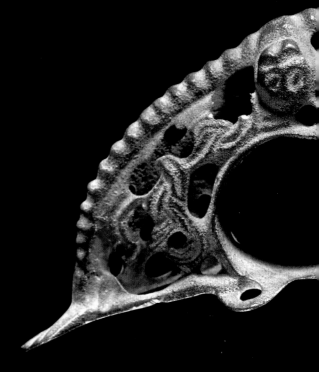

Rein-holder, with cast animal and interlace
decoration. Copper alloy, Gotland, Sweden,
10th century. Length 13.1 cm. British Museum
1921,1101.282. Purchased with contribution
from The Art Fund.

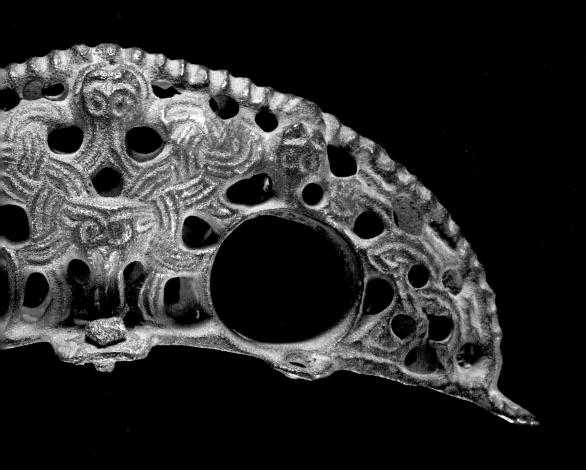

Magnus 'Barelegs' Olafsson,
king of Norway (11th century)
Magnus falls in love in Dublin

What's this talk of going home?
My heart is in Dublin,
and the women of Trondheim
won't see me this autumn.
The girl has not denied me
pleasure-visits, I'm glad;
I love the Irish lady
as well as my young self.

Silver bossed penannular brooch in the
Irish tradition, with animal heads detail.
9th–10th century, found at Goldsborough,
North Yorkshire, England. Diameter 8.5 cm.
British Museum 1859,0511.2.

Anonymous (10th century)
Ingolf is popular with the ladies

All the grown girls wanted
to go with Ingolf,
those who were of age;
the wee ones were wretched.
'I, too,' said the old woman,
'want to go with Ingolf,
as long as I have two teeth
still wobbling in my gums.'

Gilt copper-alloy oval brooch with animal interlace decoration. Uppland, Sweden, 10th century. Length 10.6 cm. British Museum 1921,1101.283, purchased with contribution from The Art Fund.

Anonymous, from the Poetic Edda
The god Odin lusts after the giant Billing's daughter

Only the mind knows what lives near the heart,
he's alone with his soul,
no sickness is worse to that wise man
than not being content.

That I discovered when sitting in the reeds,
waiting for my love;
the clever girl was my flesh and heart,
yet I couldn't have her.

Billing's daughter I found in bed,
sleeping, bright as the sun;
it was no life of a lord for me
unless I could be beside that body.

William Hamilton (1750–1801), illustration to
Thomas Gray's *Descent of Odin*. Etching and
engraving (print on paper), London, 1776.
14.3 x 9.7 cm. British Museum 1879,1109.69.

Anonymous, from the Poetic Edda
Insults among the gods: Loki accuses both
Frigg and Freyja of adultery

Be silent Frigg! You're Fjorgyn's girl
and have always been frisky,
when you, wife of Vidrir, let Vei and Vili
both embrace you.

Be silent Freyja! I know you full well,
you're not without faults;
every one of the gods and elves here
has had it off with you!

Constantin Hansen, *Ægirs Gjæstebud* (Ægir's
Banquet). Thor attacks Loki for insulting the
gods and goddesses. Lithograph on a sheet of
chine appliqué, Danish, c.1840s. 35.7 x 54.2 cm.
British Museum 1859,1210.847.

Egil Skallagrimsson (10th century)
The poet is past it

I've a crick in my neck,
and tend to fall on my head,
my trouser-snake is soft,
and my hearing's gone away.

trouser-snake = penis

Silver penny issued by Sihtric I of Northumbria (c.921–6). Part of the Vale of York Hoard, North Yorkshire, England. It was buried shortly after Sihtric's death, following the conquest of Viking Northumbria by Athelstan of Wessex (924–39). According to Egils saga, Egill Skallagrimsson served in Athelstan's campaigns in northern England.. British Museum 2009,4133.672. Jointly acquired with the Yorkshire Museums Trust.

Anonymous, from the Poetic Edda
The god Freyr falls in love with the giant
Gymir's daughter Gerd

In Gymir's gardens I saw
a girl just for me;
her arms shone, and from them
all the air and all the sea.

That girl is more mine than any other
young man's, from days of yore;
not one of the gods or elves want
us to be together.

William Gershom Collingwood (1854–1932), the
goddess Gerd. Illustration (print on paper) for
O. Bray, *The Elder or Poetic Edda*, London, 1908.

Anonymous (12th–13th century)
Love-messages on rune-sticks from
Bergen, Norway

Think of me, I'll think of you.
Love me, I'll love you.

I so love that man's wife
that fire is cold to me.
I'm that woman's friend.

Wise filigree-Var
makes me sit about in gloom.
The Eir of fishes' ground
often keeps me awake.

filigree-Var (a goddess) = woman; *fishes' ground* = sea,
its *Eir* (a goddess) = woman

Silver pendant, Scandinavia, 10th century.
4.2 x 3.7 cm. British Museum 1999,1001.1.

*Rognvald Kali Kolsson, Earl of Orkney
(12th century)*

*The poet thinks that the Viscountess
Ermengard of Narbonne is more beautiful
than northern women*

It's a fact, wise woman,
that your hair is prettier
than that of the ladies
with locks like Frodi's meal.
The prop of the hawk-field
lets hair like golden silk
fall onto her shoulders;
I redden the eagle's claws.

Frodi's meal = gold; *hawk-field* = arm, resting-place of the
hawk, its *prop* = woman; *redden the eagle's claws* = provide
the eagle with food in the form of corpses

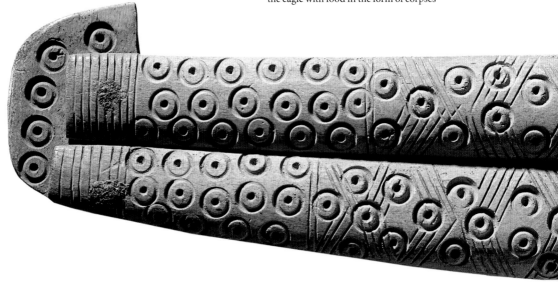

Comb-case with incised decoration. Bone,
10th–11th centuries, found in Lincoln, England.
Length 18.8 cm. British Museum 1867,0320.13.

Armod (12th century)
This poet is also smitten by Ermengard

I'll never meet Ermengard
again, unless fate says
otherwise; many men sigh
over the wise lady.
I'd be blessed if I could sleep
just one night beside her;
that would be a stroke of luck;
the lady's brow is lovely.

A heartfelt greeting. *King Sigurd*, after Edward
Burne-Jones (1833–98). Illustration (wood-
engraving) to *Good Words*, published in
London, 1862. 15.3 x 11.4 cm. British Museum
1919,0806.7.

Tindr Hallkelsson (10th century)
Earl Hakon Sigurdarson's deeds at the
Battle of Hjorungavag (c.985) are not like
going to bed with a woman

Not like when a beautiful
fire-goddess with bent shoulder-limbs
made for the earl a bed
(din of Odin's fires increased)
when he cast off the few-ringed
resounding shirt of Odin;
the steeds of the sea-leagues
were cleared of mail-coat trees.

fire-goddess = woman; *shoulder-limbs* = arms; *Odin's fires* =
swords, their *din* = battle; *shirt of Odin* = mail-coat; *steeds
of the sea-leagues* = ships; *mail-coat trees* = warriors

Gold brooch with a design of a coiled, ribbon
animal in combat with a snake. Anglo-Scandinavian,
late 11th century, found in Pitney, England. Diameter
3.9 cm. British Museum 1979,1101.1.

Anonymous, from the Poetic Edda
The valkyrie Sigrun visits her dead lover
Helgi in his burial mound

Sigrun:
I'm looking forward to our meeting
like Odin's carrion-eager hawks,
dew-coloured, looking at daybreak,
knowing there'll be corpses, warm morsels.

I want to kiss the lifeless king
before you throw off your bloody byrnie;
your hair, Helgi, is frost-matted,
the captain is sprinkled with corpse-dew,
Hogni's son-in-law has rain-cool hands;
how, o prince, shall I repair this for you?

Helgi:
You alone, Sigrun from the Sefafells,
caused Helgi to be sprinkled with corpse-dew;
gold-adorned you weep with grim tears,
sun-bright, southern, before you sleep;
each falls, bloody, on the prince's breast,
rain-cool, burning inside, sorrow-clenched.

Odin's hawks = ravens; *corpse-dew* = blood

Thomas Fearnley (1802–1842), a burial
mound in Sognefjord, Norway. Etching,
Norwegian, 1838–1842. 13.8 x 17.8 cm.
British Musuem 1926,0331.689. Donated
by James R. Saunders.

Rognvald Kali Kolsson, Earl of Orkney
(12th century)
In the midst of battle, the poet
remembers his lady love

The pure, white headband-Nipt
of forearm-snow brought us wine;
the guys could see Ermengard's
beauty when we met.
Sharp swords swing from scabbards
now, as the staunchly bold
guys get ready to attack
this castle here with fire.

headband-Nipt (goddess) *of forearm-snow* (gold) = woman

Gold arm-ring made of thick and thin
wires twisted together. 10th century.
Diameter 8.8 cm. British Museum
1849,0210.1. Donated by G. Robert Fox.

Anonymous, from the Prose Edda
Marital difficulties of the sea-god Njord and the
mountain-giantess Skadi

Njord:
I'm fed up of the fells, I wasn't there for long,
nine nights only;
the howling of wolves seemed far worse to me
than the song of swans.

Skadi:
I just can't fall asleep beside the sea
for the screeching of birds;
he wakes me every morning, the seagull
coming from the waves.

Queen chess piece from the Lewis Chessmen.
Walrus ivory chess pieces, probably made in
Norway, c.1150–1175; found on the Isle of Lewis,
Scotland. Height 9.6 cm. British Museum
1831,1101.84.

Anonymous, from the Poetic Edda
Volund and his brothers fall in love

Maidens flew north, across Mirkwood,
young, strange creatures, to fulfil their fate;
they sat down to rest beside the lake,
southern ladies, spinning fine linen.

One of them, a lovely human maiden,
drew Egil to her fair bosom;
the second was Swan-white, wearing swan's plumage;
and their sister, the third one, threw
her arms around Volund's neck.

The Franks Casket (detail). Rectangular whale-bone box, carved in relief with scenes from Roman, Jewish, Christian and Germanic tradition. Here, a figure is shown catching swans. Northumbria, England, early 8th century. Length 23 cm; width 19 cm; height 13 cm. British Museum 1867,0120.1. Donated by Sir Augustus Wollaston Franks.

Anonymous, from the Poetic Edda
Volund takes his revenge on King Nidud's family by killing their sons

One boy called to the other, quickly,
brother to brother, let's go look at the ring!

They went to the chest, demanded the keys,
evil was obvious, when they looked in;
he cut off the heads of those lads,
and laid their legs in the smithy's mess;
and those bowls which held their hair,
he covered with silver and gave to Nidud.

And he sent the jewels of their eyes
to Nidud's knowing wife;
and from the teeth of those two
he made brooches for Bodvild.

bowls which held their hair = skulls

The Franks Casket (detail). Rectangular whale-bone box, carved in relief with scenes from Roman, Jewish, Christian and Germanic tradition. Here, Volund the Smith is shown holding the head of one of the princes in his smith's tongs, and a cup made from the skull of the other prince, whose decapitated body lies at his feet. Northumbria, England, early 8th century. Length 23 cm; width 19 cm; height 13 cm. British Museum 1867,0120.1. Donated by Sir Augustus Wollaston Franks.

Anonymous, from the Poetic Edda
*Gudrun, daughter of Gjuki, learns of the killing of
her husband Sigurd by her brothers at the assembly*

Sigurd was superior to the sons of Gjuki
like the green leek to other grasses,
or a long-legged stag to stockier beasts,
or red-glowing gold to the hoar of silver.

Until my brothers begrudged me
my marriage to the best of all men,
they could not sleep, nor settle matters
before they caused Sigurd's killing.

Grani galloped from the meeting with great noise,
but Sigurd himself did not come,
the saddle-beast was blood-besprinkled,
and badly treated by those butchers.

Weeping I went to converse with Grani,
wet-cheeked, I asked the steed for news,
despondent Grani's head drooped to the grass,
the steed knew that his master was dead.

saddle-beast = horse

Illustration (wood-engraving after Edward
Burne-Jones (1833–98)) to *The Story of Sigurd
the Volsung*, published by The Kelmscott Press,
London, 1896. 22.2 x 15.9 cm. British Museum
1912,0612.396.

Tjorvi Hroarsson (10th century)
In his jealousy, Tjorvi makes images of his
beloved, Astrid, now married to Thorir

Spindle-whorl with beads of glass and
amber. Gotland, Sweden, 11th–12th
century. British Museum 1921,1101.53.
Purchased with contribution from
The Art Fund.

I've painted a picture
of the wealthy young woman
on the wall, and Thorir's too;
that was out of mischief.
On my knife's handle I've carved
the goddess of the ale-keg;
I've cast the evil eye
on the bright amber-girl.

goddess of the ale-keg = woman; *amber-girl* =
woman wearing amber jewellery

Hallbjorn Oddsson (10th century)
Hallbjorn berates his wife Hallgerd for
refusing to go home with him, before
cutting off her head

The goddess of ale-mugs,
in headdress of linen,
makes a fool out of me,
I hate the oak of arms.
Never will my bride
make things better for me,
misery makes me pale,
the grief attacks my heart.

goddess of ale-mugs = woman; *oak of arms* = woman

Gold finger-ring, 9th–10th century. Found at
Maunby, North Yorkshire, England. Diameter
2.2 cm. British Museum 2009,8001.1.

Anonymous, from the Poetic Edda
*Be cautious in your praise and appropriate
in your actions*

Praise the day at evening,
the wife when she's cremated,
a sword when it's tested,
a girl when she's married,
ice when you've crossed it,
beer when you've drunk it.

Chop wood in the wind,
row out to sea in good weather,
speak to a girl in the dark;
the day's eyes are many;
you need a ship for gliding,
a shield for protection,
a sword for striking,
a maiden for kissing.

William Gershom Collingwood (1854–1932),
Day-Spring and Menglod. Illustration (print
on paper) for O. Bray, *The Elder* or *Poetic Edda*,
London, 1908.

Biographical notes

ADILS tenth-century Welsh earl, brother of Hring.

ARMOD twelfth-century Icelandic poet, associate of Rognvald.

ARNOR 'EARLS'-POET' THORDARSON eleventh-century Icelandic poet;
    worked for the kings of Norway and the earls of Orkney.

ASTRID MODOLFSDOTTIR tenth-century Icelander, beloved of Tjorvi, married to Thorir.

ATHELSTAN tenth-century king of England.

EGIL SKALLAGRIMSSON tenth-century Icelandic warrior and poet, hero of *Egils saga*.

EINAR SIGURDARSON brother of, and joint Earl of Orkney with, Thorfinn.

EINAR SKULASON twelfth-century Icelandic priest and poet.

EIRIK 'BLOODAXE' HARALDSSON tenth-century king of Norway who also ruled in York.

ERMENGARD twelfth-century Viscountess of Narbonne in Provence.

FRODI OGMUNDARSON tenth-century Icelander, brother of Kormak.

GRANI eleventh-century poet.

HAKON SIGURDARSON tenth-century Norwegian earl.

HALLBJORN ODDSSON tenth-century Icelander.

HALLGERD TUNGU-ODDSDOTTIR wife of Hallbjorn.

HALLFRED 'THE TROUBLESOME POET' OTTARSSON tenth-century Icelandic poet and
    hero of *Hallfreðar saga*.

HARALD 'THE HARD-RULER' SIGURDARSON king of Norway 1046–66; fought at the battle
    of Stiklestad in 1030; spent some years in Novgorod and Byzantium as a successful
    mercenary; as king of Norway fought against the Danes; died at Stamford Bridge
    in 1066.

HRING tenth-century Welsh earl, brother of Adils.

INGIGERD OLAFSDOTTIR eleventh-century Swedish princess.

INGOLF THORSTEINSSON tenth-century Icelander, 'the handsomest man in the
    north of Iceland'.

INGVAR eleventh-century Swede whose disastrous expedition to the east is
    commemorated on some thirty rune stones.

Kolfinna beloved of Hallfred.

Kormak Ogmundarson tenth-century Icelandic poet and hero of *Kormáks saga*.

Kveld-Ulf Bjalfason ninth-/tenth-century Norwegian chieftain, grandfather of Egil.

Magnus 'the Good' Olafsson king of Norway 1035–47; ruled jointly with his uncle Harald and fought several campaigns in the Baltic.

Magnus 'Barelegs' Olafsson king of Norway 1093–1103; died on a raid in Ireland.

Olaf 'the Red' tenth-century Scottish king.

Olaf Haraldsson king of Norway 1015–1028, died at Stiklestad in 1030, subsequently canonized.

Rognvald Kali Kolsson Earl of Orkney, d. *c.*1158; renowned for his journey to the Holy Land, during which he stopped off in Narbonne, Provence and composed about the Viscountess Ermengard.

Steingerd beloved of Kormak.

Thjodolf Arnorsson eleventh-century Icelandic poet; worked for the kings of Norway.

Thorfinn Sigurdarson eleventh-century Earl of Orkney.

Thorir Ketilsson husband of Astrid.

Thorolf Kveld-Ulfsson Uncle of Egil.

Tindr Hallkelsson tenth-century Icelandic poet.

Tjorvi 'the Spiteful' Hroarsson tenth-century Icelander.

Mythological names

AUSTRI one of the four dwarves holding up the sky.

BALDR Odin's son.

BILLING giant.

BODVILD daughter of Nidud, raped by Volund.

BRAGI god of poetry.

EGIL brother of Volund.

EINHERJAR the warriors of Valhalla.

EIR goddess of medicine.

FJORGYN father of Frigg.

FREYJA goddess of love, sister of Freyr.

FREYR god of fertility, brother of Freyja.

FRIGG goddess, wife of Odin.

FRODI legendary Danish king, who had a magic mill that ground out gold.

GERD giantess, daughter of Gymir.

GJUKI father of Gudrun and her brothers.

GRANI Sigurd's horse.

GUDRUN GJUKADOTTIR legendary heroine, married to Sigurd.

GUNN valkyrie.

GYMIR giant, father of Gerd.

HEL offspring of Loki, presides over the world of the dead.

HELGI HUNDINGSBANI legendary hero, beloved of Sigrun.

HLIN goddess of protection.

HLOKK valkyrie

HOGNI father of Sigrun.

HOGNI GJUKASON legendary warrior referred to in kennings for 'battle' and 'weapons'.

HUGIN one of Odin's ravens.

LOKI son of a giant, troublesome friend and enemy of the gods, sometimes considered one of the gods.

MEITI sea-king.

MIRKWOOD a large forest in the south.

NARI son of Loki, half-brother of Hel.

NIDUD legendary king, tormentor of Volund.

NIPT goddess or norn.

NJORD god of the sea, father of Freyja and Freyr.

NORN female supernatural being who decides fate.

ODIN chief of the gods, god of war and ruler of Valhalla.

SAGA goddess.

SEFAFELLS home of Sigrun.

SIGRUN valkyrie, beloved of Helgi.

SIGURD legendary hero, married to Gudrun, killed by her brothers.

SKADI giantess, married to Njord.

SWAN-WHITE one of three swan-maidens beloved by Volund and his brothers.

VALHALLA home of Odin and his select dead warriors.

VALKYRIES Odin's female assistants and/or warrior-maidens.

VAR goddess of oaths.

VEI brother of Odin.

VIDRIR another name for Odin.

VILI brother of Odin.

VOLUND legendary craftsman, deserted by his swan-maiden, captured and maimed by Nidud, on whose family he takes various forms of revenge.

Geographical names

BERGEN town in western Norway.
DUBLIN town in Ireland.
GUDENÅ large river in Denmark.
HJORUNGAVAG unidentified bay in north-west Norway.
JUTISH from Jutland, Denmark.
LONDON town in England.
LUND town in southern Sweden.
NID river from which Nidaros (modern Trondheim) takes its name.
SARACENLAND somewhere in Russia or further east.
STAMFORD BRIDGE site of Harald Sigurdarson's final battle, near York.
STIKLESTAD site of Olaf Haraldsson's final battle, near Trondheim.
TRONDHEIM town in Norway.
UTSTEIN just outside Bergen.

Further reading

In compiling this anthology, I have consulted the following editions and translations:

Jakob Benediktsson, *Íslendingabók, Landnámabók* (Hið íslenzka fornritafélag, 1968).

Ursula Dronke, *The Poetic Edda I-III* (Oxford University Press, 1969–2011).

Bjarni Einarsson, *Egils saga* (Viking Society for Northern Research, 2003).

Anthony Faulkes, *Snorri Sturluson. Edda: Prologue and Gylfaginning* (Oxford University Press, 1982).

Anthony Faulkes, *Snorri Sturluson. Edda* (Everyman, 1987).

Kari Ellen Gade, *Poetry from the Kings' Sagas 2* (Brepols, 2009).

Judith Jesch, *Women in the Viking Age* (Boydell, 1991).

Beatrice La Farge and John Tucker, *Glossary to the Poetic Edda* (Carl Winter, 1992).

Carolyne Larrington, *The Poetic Edda* (Oxford University Press, 1996).

Gustav Neckel and Hans Kuhn, *Edda. Die Lieder des Codex Regius nebst verwandten Denkmälern* (Carl Winter, 1983).

Andy Orchard, *The Elder Edda: A Book of Viking Lore* (Penguin, 2011).

Hermann Pálsson and Paul Edwards, *The Book of Settlements. Landnámabók* (University of Manitoba Press, 1972).

Einar Ólafur Sveinsson, *Vatnsdœla saga, Hallfreðar saga, Kormáks saga* (Hið íslenzka fornritafélag, 1939).

Diana Whaley, *Sagas of Warrior-Poets* (Penguin, 2002).

Diana Whaley, *Poetry from the Kings' Sagas 1* (Brepols, 2012).

Recommended reading on Old Norse poetry and its literary and historical background:

Stefan Brink with Neil Price, *The Viking World* (Routledge, 2008).
Sven B. F. Jansson, *Runes in Sweden* (Gidlunds, 1987).
Rory McTurk, *A Companion to Old Norse-Icelandic Literature and Culture*
    (Blackwell, 2005).
Margaret Clunies Ross, *A History of Old Norse Poetry and Poetics* (D.S. Brewer, 2005).
Margaret Clunies Ross, *The Cambridge Introduction to the Old Norse-Icelandic Saga*
    (Cambridge University Press, 2010).
Terje Spurkland, *Norwegian Runes and Runic Inscriptions* (Boydell, 2005).

Web resources:

The Uppsala Runic Forum
    http://www.runforum.nordiska.uu.se
This site provides links to many useful resources on runes, as well as the Scandinavian
Runic-text Database.

Skaldic Poetry of the Scandinavian Middle Ages
    http://homepages.abdn.ac.uk/wag017/db.php

The British Museum collection online
The majority of artworks illustrated in this book are from the collection of the British
Museum. The registration numbers for these objects are provided in the corresponding
captions. To find out more about these and objects in all areas of the British Museum's
collection, visit: britishmuseum.org/research/search_the_collection_database.aspx.

Picture credits

Every effort has been made to trace the copyright holders of the images reproduced in this book. Unless otherwise stated below, all of the photographs are © The Trustees of the British Museum and courtesy of the Museum's Department of Photography and Imaging.

Page

6   © Bibliothèque Nationale, Paris
18   © Stan Pritchard
33   Photo: akg-images
37   Photo: The Bridgeman Art Library
48   Photo: The Bridgeman Art Library
55   © The British Library Board
61   Photo: Werner Karrasch/
     © The Viking Ship Museum, Denmark
63   Photo: the author
77   © The British Library Board
102 © The British Library Board